Rib It Up ™

Designs by Frances Hughes and Sue Childress

HOUSE of
WHITE
BIRCHES

PUBLISHERS
SINCE 1947

Table of Contents

Chevron Rib Place Mat,
page 26

Little Chevron Rib Afghan,
page 7

Wavy Rib Hand Towel
& Dishcloth,
page 22

Diamond Rib
Cloth & Towel,
page 16

Pretty Posies Tea Cozy,
page 38

Mock-Cable Rib
Hand Towel,
page 24

Introduction

Exploring the world of rib patterns sounds like a great idea. Fill your home with projects made exclusively with rib knit patterns. I never realized how versitile rib patterns were until the idea of home decor projects came to mind. There seems to be an endless selection of patterns to use, and with each item comes an idea for another.

These patterns will delight the beginner and the experienced knitter. The 20+ patterns are geared to many ideas for our homes and even more gift ideas. Be sure to change the colors to meet your individual needs. Happy exploring!

Meet the Designers

Frances Hughes

I was born in a small town in East Texas, and I am 75 years young. My husband and I have been married since 1952. We have two sons, nine adult grandchildren and eight great-grandchildren.

I learned to crochet at a very young age. Being left-handed made this a challenge, but the rewards far outweighed the effort it took. Then, much later in life, I learned to knit. Knitting opened up a whole new way of expressing myself through my needlecrafting, broadening my horizons.

My sister Sue and I opened a yarn shop in 1984. It has been plenty of fun and quite a bit of work, but I love it all. I sold my first design to Annie's Attic in 1984 after telling Sue that if she could do that, I could too.

Sue and I have had designs published by Annie's Attic, Needlecraft Shop, House of White Birches and Leisure Arts. My designs have also been in several magazines, including *Knitting Digest, Creative Knitting, Crochet World, Old-Time Crochet, McCalls, Country Woman* and *Ribbon Works*.

Sue Childress

I was born in a very small town to a mother who loved crafts and crochet. I've been married to Robert since 1957. We have two children and five grandchildren.

When my children were small, I would ask them if they liked what I was making. If they said no, then I would never make that item again. When my sister Frances and I were attending craft fairs, my daughter was a good gauge for us. If she liked a project, it was always a best-seller.

My sister and I opened Stitches 'N Stuff Yarn and Gift Shop in 1984. I have enjoyed being a part of the yarn industry with all its ups and downs. I never get tired of all the wonderful yarns and notions that have flooded our world over the last few years.

I've known how to crochet since I was a little girl, but I didn't learn to knit until I was 54. I've enjoyed knitting as much as crocheting. It's much more fun to know how to do both!

House of White Birches, Berne, Indiana 46711   AnniesAttic.com

Cable & Eyelet Rib Afghan

Design by Frances Hughes

Skill Level

 INTERMEDIATE

Finished Size
42 x 54 inches

Materials
- Plymouth Baby Alpaca Grande (bulky weight; 100% baby alpaca; 110 yds/100g per skein): 9 skeins tan #202
- Size 10½ (6.5mm) 29-inch circular needle or size needed to obtain gauge
- Cable needle
- Stitch markers

Gauge
12 sts and 16 rows = 4 inches/10cm in St st.
To save time, take time to check gauge.

Special Abbreviation
Cable 4 Front (C4F): Slip next 4 sts onto cn and hold to front of work, k2 from LH needle, k4 from cn.

Pattern Stitch
Cable & Eyelet Rib

Row 1 (RS): [K2, p2] 4 times, k2tog, yo, *p2, k4, p2, k2tog, yo; rep from * to last 16 sts, p1, k1, [p2, k2] 3 times, p2.

Row 2: [K2, p2] 3 times, k2, p1, k1, p2, *k2, p4, k2, p2; rep from * to last 16 sts, [k2, p2] 4 times.

Row 3: [P2, k2] 3 times, p2, k1, p1, yo, ssk, *p2, C4F, p2, yo, ssk; rep from * across to last 16 sts, [p2, k2] 4 times.

Row 4: [P2, k2] 4 times, p2, *k2, p4, k2, p2; rep from * to last 16 sts, k1, p1, [p2, k2] 3 times, k2.

Row 5: [K2, p2] 4 times, k2tog, yo, *p2, k4, p2, k2tog, yo; rep from * to last 16 sts, p1, k1, [p2, k2] 3 times, p2.

Row 6: [K2, p2] 3 times, k2, p1, k1, p2, *k2, p4, k2, p2; rep from * to last 16 sts, [k2, p2] 4 times.

Row 7: [P2, k2] 3 times, p2, k1, p1, yo, ssk, *p2, k4, p2, yo, ssk; rep from * to last 16 sts, [p2, k2] 4 times.

Row 8: [P2, k2] 4 times, p2, *k2, p4, k2, p2; rep from * to last 16 sts, k1, p1, [k2, p2] 3 times, k2.

Rep Rows 1–8 for pat.

Pattern Notes
Circular needle is used to accommodate stitches. Do not join; work back and forth in rows.

It may be helpful to place a marker after the first 16 stitches and before the last 16 stitches for ease in recognizing the border stitches when working the Cable & Eyelet Rib pattern.

continued on page 41

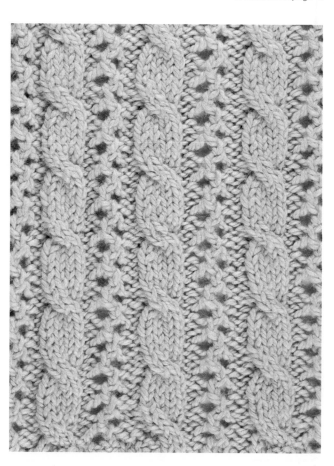

Little Chevron Rib Afghan

Design by Frances Hughes

Skill Level

 ◼◼◻◻ EASY

Finished Size

44 x 62 inches, after blocking

Materials

- Berroco Peruvia Quick (bulky weight; 100% Peruvian highland wool; 103 yds/ 100g per hank): 9 hanks blanco #9100
- Size 11 (8mm) 32-inch circular needle or size needed to obtain gauge

Gauge

12 sts and 16 rows = 4 inches/10cm in Chevron Rib pat.
To save time, take time to check gauge.

Pattern Stitch

Chevron Rib

Row 1 (RS): K1, [yo, k2tog] 6 times, p1, *k1, p1, [k2, p1] twice, k1, p1; rep from * to last 13 sts, [k2tog, yo] 6 times, k1.

Row 2: P13, k1, *p2, [k1, p1] twice, k1, p2, k1; rep from * to last 13 sts, p13.

Row 3: K1, [yo, k2tog] 6 times, p1, *k3, p3, k3, p1; rep from * to last 13 sts, [k2tog, yo] 6 times, k1.

Row 4: P13, k2, [p3, k1, p3, k3] 7 times, p3, k1, p3, k2, p13.

Rep Rows 1–4 for pat.

Afghan

Cast on 107 sts.

Border

Row 1: K1, *yo, k2tog; rep from * across.

Row 2: Purl across.

Rep [Rows 1 and 2] 7 times.

Body

Work [Rows 1–4 of Chevron Rib pat] 38 times.

Border

Row 1: K1, *yo, k2tog; rep from * across.

Row 2: Purl across.

Rep [Rows 1 and 2] 7 times, then rep Row 1.

Bind off loosely purlwise. Block as desired. ❖

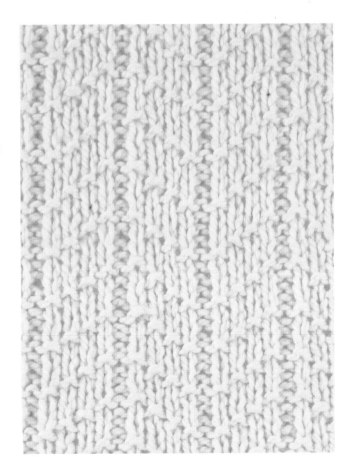

Bobble Rib Bolster

Design by Frances Hughes

Skill Level

 ■■□□ EASY

Finished Size
20 inches long x 19 inches around

Materials
- Berroco Peruvia Quick (bulky weight; 100% Peruvian highland wool; 103 yds/100g per hank): 3 hanks blanco #9100
- Size 10½ (6.5mm) needles or size needed to obtain gauge
- Bolster pillow form
- 2 (1½-inch) round shank buttons

Gauge
16 sts = 4 inches/10cm in St st.
To save time, take time to check gauge.

Special Abbreviation
Make Bobble (MB): Work (p1, k1, p1, k1) all in next st, sl 2nd, 3rd and 4th sts over first st to complete bobble.

Bolster
Cast on 75 sts.

Row 1: K8, p3, [yo, k1, yo, p2] 3 times, k3, *p2, MB, p2, k3; rep from * 3 times, p2, [yo, k1, yo, p2] 3 times, p1, k8—87 sts.

Row 2: P8, k3, [p3, k2] 3 times, p3, [k5, p3] 4 times, k2, [p3, k2] 3 times, k1, p8.

Row 3: K8, p3, [k3, p2] 3 times, k3, [p5, k3] 4 times, p2, [k3, p2] 3 times, p1, k8.

Row 4: P8, k3, [p3tog, k2] 3 times, p3, [k5, p3] 4 times, k2, [p3tog, k2] 3 times, k1, p8—75 sts.

Work [Rows 1–4] 18 times or until piece measures about 19 inches. Bind off.

Finishing
Sew cast-on and bound-off edges tog. Insert pillow form. Run gathering thread through sts at each end and draw up to close. Sew button in center of each end. ❖

Sailor's Rib Pillow

Design by Sue Childress

Skill Level

 EASY

Finished Size
14 inches square

Materials
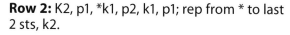
- Berroco Peruvia Quick (bulky weight; 100% Peruvian highland wool; 103 yds/100g per hank): 2 hanks aquamarina #9143
- Size 11 (8mm) needles or size needed to obtain gauge
- 14-inch pillow form

Gauge
12 sts and 14 rows = 4 inches/10cm in Sailor Rib pat. To save time, take time to check gauge.

Pattern Stitch
Sailor Rib

Row 1 (RS): K2, k1-tbl, *p1, k2, p1, k1-tbl; rep from * to last 2 sts, k2.

Row 2: K2, p1, *k1, p2, k1, p1; rep from * to last 2 sts, k2.

Row 3: K2, k1-tbl, *p4, k1-tbl; rep from * to last 2 sts, k2.

Row 4: K2, p1, *k4, p1; rep from * to last 2 sts, k2.

Rep Rows 1–4 for pat.

Pillow

Front/Back
Cast on 45 sts. Knit 2 rows.

Work Rows 1–4 of Sailor Rib pat until piece measures about 13½ inches.

Knit 2 rows. Bind off.

Finishing
Hold Front and Back with RS tog. Sew along 3 sides. Turn to RS, insert pillow form and sew rem side. ❖

Broken Rib Doily

Design by Frances Hughes

Skill Level

 INTERMEDIATE

Finished Size

11 inches square

Materials

- Omega 5 (size 5 crochet cotton; 164 yds/ 50g per ball): 1 ball pink #56
- Size 7 (4.5mm) needles or size needed to obtain gauge
- Stitch markers

Gauge

24 sts and 28 rows = 4 inches/10cm in St st.
To save time, take time to check gauge.

Special Abbreviation

Make 5 (M5): Work (k1, yo, k1, yo, k1) all in next st making 5 sts from 1 st.

Doily

Cast on 80 sts.

Border

Row 1 (WS): K1, *p5tog, M5; rep from * to last st, k1.

Row 2 (RS): K1, purl to last st, k1.

Row 3: K1, *M5, p5tog; rep from * to last st, k1.

Row 4: K1, purl to last st, k1.

Row 5: K1, *k1, yo; rep from * to last st, k1.

Row 6: K1, purl to last st dropping yo's, k1.

Rows 7–18: Rep [Rows 1–6] twice.

Row 19: K1, *p5tog, M5; rep from * to last st, k1.

Body

Row 1 (RS): K1, p18, place marker, *k4, p2; rep from * to last 19 sts, place marker, p18, k1.

Row 2: K1, [M5, p5tog] 3 times, *k2, p4; rep from * to marker, [M5, p5tog] 3 times, k1.

Row 3: K1, p18, *k4, p2; rep from * to marker, p18, k1.

Row 4: K1, [k1, yo] to marker, *k2, p4; rep from * to marker, [yo, k1] to last st, k1.

Row 5: K1, purl to marker dropping yo's, k2, *p2, k4; rep from * to 4 sts before marker, p2, k2, purl to last st dropping yo's, k1.

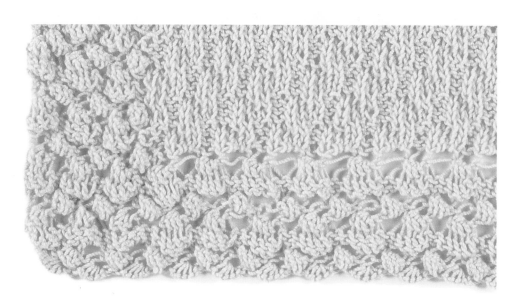

Row 6: K1, [p5tog, M5] 3 times, p2, *k2, p4; rep from * to 4 sts before marker, k2, p2, [p5tog, M5] 3 times, k1.

Row 7: K1, p18, k2, *p2, k4; rep from * to 4 sts before marker, p2, k2, p18, k1.

Row 8: K1, [M5, p5tog] 3 times, p1, *k2, p4; rep from * to 4 sts before marker, k2, p2, [M5, p5tog] 3 times, k1.

Row 9: K1, p18, *p2, k4; rep from * to marker, p18, k1.

Row 10: K1, [k1, yo] 18 times, *p4, k2; rep from * to marker, [yo, k1] 18 times, k1.

Row 11: K1, purl to marker dropping yo's, *p2, k4; rep from * to marker, purl to last st dropping yo's, k1.

Row 12: K1, [p5tog, M5] 3 times, *p4, k2; rep from * to marker, [p5tog, M5] 3 times, k1.

Rep [Rows 1–12] twice, then rep Rows 1–5.

Border

Row 1: K1, *p5tog, M5; rep from * to last st, k1.

Row 2: K1, purl to last st, k1.

Row 3: K1, *M5, p5tog; rep from * to last st, k1.

Row 4: K1, purl to last st, k1.

Row 5: K1, *k1, yo; rep from * to last st, k1.

Row 6: K1, purl to last st dropping yo's, k1.

Rep [Rows 1–6] twice.

Bind off.

Block if necessary. ❖

Fancy Slip-Stitch Rib Rug

Design by Sue Childress

Skill Level

 EASY

Finished Size
24 x 35 inches, after blocking

Materials
- Kertzer Marble Chunky (chunky weight; 100% acrylic; 341 yds/200g per ball): 2 skeins adobe #16
- Size 13 (9mm) needles or size needed to obtain gauge

5 BULKY

Gauge
10 sts and 18 rows = 4 inches/10cm in St st with 2 strands of yarn held tog.
To save time, take time to check gauge.

Pattern Stitch
Fancy Slip-Stitch Rib

Row 1: K2, p5, *k1, sl 1p wyif, k1, p2; rep from * to last 5 sts, p3, k2.

Row 2: P2, k5, *p3, k2; rep from * to last 5 sts, k3, p2.

Rep Rows 1 and 2 for pat.

Rug
With 2 strands of yarn held tog, cast on 62 sts.

Border
Row 1 (RS): *K2, p3; rep from * to last 2 sts, k2.

Row 2: *P2, k3; rep from * to last 2 sts, p2.

Rep [Rows 1 and 2] 3 times.

Body
Work Rows 1 and 2 of Fancy Slip-Stitch Rib pat until rug measures about 33 inches, ending with Row 2.

Border
Row 1: *K2, p3; rep from * to last 2 sts, k2.

Row 2: *P2, k3; rep from * to last 2 sts, p2.

Rep [Rows 1 and 2] 3 times.

Bind off in pat.

Wet-block to measurements.

To wet-block: Wet item completely with water, roll in a towel to remove excess moisture. Place flat, shaping to measurements. Let dry completely. ❖

House of White Birches, Berne, Indiana 46711   AnniesAttic.com

Diamond Rib Cloth & Towel

Designs by Sue Childress

Skill Level

◼◼◻◻ EASY

Finished Sizes
Cloth: 9½ inches square
Towel: 19 x 26 inches, after wet blocking

Materials
- Plymouth Fantasy Naturale (worsted weight; 100% cotton; 140 yds/100g per skein): 3 skeins fuchsia #9004
- Size 9 (5.5mm) 24-inch circular needle

Gauge
16 sts = 4 inches/10cm in garter st; 3 reps of Rows 1–8 of pat = 4 inches.
To save time, take time to check gauge.

Pattern Stitch
Diamond Rib

Row 1 (RS): K4, p2, *k2tog, [k1, yo] twice, k1, ssk, p2; rep from * to last 4 sts, k4.

Row 2 and all even-number rows: K6, *p7, k2; rep from * to last 4 sts, k4.

Row 3: K4, p2, *k2tog, yo, k3, yo, ssk, p2; rep from * to last 4 sts, k4.

Row 5: K4, p2, *k1, yo, ssk, k1, k2tog, yo, k1, p2; rep from * to last 4 sts, k4.

Row 7: K4, p2, *k2, yo, sk2p, yo, k2, p2; rep from * to last 4 sts, k4.

Row 8: K6, *p7, k2; rep from * to last 4 sts, k4.

Rep Rows 1–8 for pat.

Pattern Notes
Yarn amounts sufficient for both cloth and towel.

Circular needle is used to accommodate stitches. Do not join; work back and forth in rows.

Cloth
Cast on 37 sts. Knit 4 rows.

Work [Rows 1–8 of Diamond Rib pat] 5 times.

Knit 4 rows. Bind off.

Towel
Cast on 73 sts. Knit 4 rows.

Row [Rows 1–8 of Diamond Rib pat] 16 times.

Knit 4 rows. Bind off.

Wet-block if desired.

To wet-block: Wet item completely with water, roll in a towel to remove excess moisture. Place flat, shaping to measurements. Let dry completely. ❖

Puffed Rib Cloth & Soap Holder

Designs by Sue Childress

Skill Level

 EASY

Finished Sizes

Cloth: 10 inches square
Soap Holder: 4 x 6 inches, folded

Materials

- Reynolds Saucy (worsted weight; 100% cotton; 185 yds/100g per ball): 1 ball olive #528
- Size 9 (5.5mm) needles or size needed to obtain gauge
- Size 13 (9mm) needles
- 22 inches ¼-inch-wide satin ribbon (for soap holder)

Gauge

16 sts = 4 inches/10cm in St st with smaller needles. To save time, take time to check gauge.

Cloth

With smaller needles, cast on 37 sts.

Border

Row 1: *P1, k1; rep from * to last st, p1.

Rows 2–4: Rep Row 1.

Body

Row 1 (RS): [P1, k1] twice, p2, *yo, k1, yo, p2; rep from * to last 4 sts, [k1, p1] twice—55 sts.

Row 2: [P1, k1] twice, k2, *p3, k2; rep from * to last 4 sts, [k1, p1] twice.

Row 3: [P1, k1] twice, p2, *k3, p2; rep from * to last 4 sts, [k1, p1] twice.

Row 4: [P1, k1] twice, k2, *p3tog, k2; rep from * to last 4 sts, [k1, p1] twice—37 sts.

Rep [Rows 1–4] 9 times.

Border

Row 1: *P1, k1; rep from * to last st, p1.

Rows 2–4: Rep Row 1.

Bind off.

Wet-block, if desired, to measurements.

To wet-block: Wet item completely with water, roll in a towel to remove excess moisture. Place flat, shaping to measurements. Let dry completely.

Soap Holder
With smaller needles, cast on 26 sts.

Bottom
Row 1: *K1, p1; rep from * across.

Row 2: *P1, k1; rep from * across.

Rep [Rows 1 and 2] twice.

Body
Row 1 (RS): P2, *yo, k1, yo, p2; rep from * across—42 sts.

Row 2: K2, *p3, k2; rep from * across.

Row 3: P2, *k3, p2; rep from * across.

Row 4: K2, *p3tog, k2; rep from * across—26 sts.

Rep [Rows 1–4] 4 times.

Change to larger needles and work Rows 1–4 for top ruffle.

Bind off, cut yarn, leaving an 18-inch end for sewing.

Fold and sew side seam and across bottom.

Weave ribbon through Row 1 of ruffle and tie ends in bow. ❖

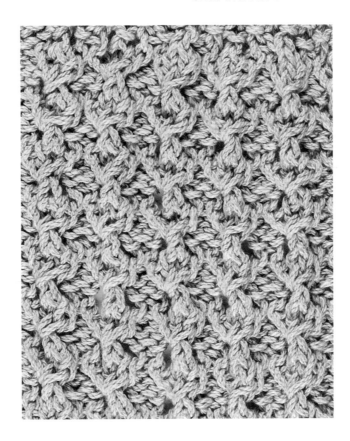

Textured Rib Washcloth & Scrub

Designs by Sue Childress

Skill Level

 EASY

Finished Sizes

Washcloth: 9 inches square
Scrub: 3½ inches across

Materials

- Reynolds Saucy (worsted weight; 100% cotton; 185 yds/100g per ball): 1 ball burgundy #703
- Size 9 (5.5mm) needles or size needed to obtain gauge

Gauge

16 sts = 4 inches/10cm in St st.
To save time, take time to check gauge.

Pattern Stitch

Textured Rib

Row 1 (WS): [K1, p1] twice, p3, *k3, p3; rep from * to last 4 sts, [p1, k1] twice.

Row 2 (RS): [K1, p1] twice, k3, *p1, sl 1k wyib, p1, k3; rep from * to last 4 sts, [p1, k1] twice.

Rows 3–6: Rep [Rows 1 and 2] twice.

Row 7: [K1, p1] twice, knit to last 4 sts, [p1, k1] twice.

Row 8: [K1, p1] twice, p4, *sl 1k wyib, p5; rep from * to last 3 sts, k1, p1, k1.

Rep Rows 1–8 for pat.

Washcloth

Cast on 41 sts.

Border

Row 1: *K1, p1; rep from * to last st, k1.

Rows 2–4: Rep Row 1.

Body

Work [Rows 1–8 of Textured Rib pat] 5 times.

Rep Rows 1–6 of pat.

Border

Row 1: *K1, p1; rep from * to last st, k1.

Rows 2–4: Rep Row 1.

Bind off.

Scrub

Cast on 41 sts.

Work [Rows 1–8 of Textured Rib pat] twice.

Next row: *P3tog; rep from * to last 2 sts, p2tog—14 sts.

Next row: *P2tog; rep from * across—7 sts.

Bind off, cut yarn leaving a 12-inch end. Weave end through bound-off sts and pull tight, then sew sides tog. Cut an 18-inch length of yarn and weave it through cast-on row, pull tight and finish off. ❖

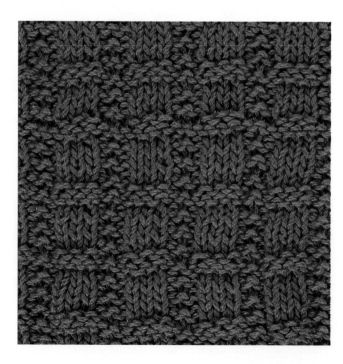

Wavy Rib Hand Towel & Dishcloth

Designs by Sue Childress

Skill Level

 EASY

Finished Sizes

Dishcloth: 9 inches square
Hand Towel: 16 x 21 inches, before buttoning

Materials

- Plymouth Fantasy Naturale (worsted weight; 100% cotton; 140 yds/100g per skein): 2 skeins autumn multi #9995
- Size 9 (5.5mm) 24-inch circular needle or size needed to obtain gauge
- 1½-inch decorative button

Gauge

16 sts = 4 inches/10cm in St st.
To save time, take time to check gauge.

Special Abbreviations

Cross 2 Front (C2F): Knit in front of 2nd st of LH needle, then knit in first st, slipping both sts from needle tog.

Cross 2 Back (C2B): Knit in back of 2nd st of LH needle, then knit in first st, slipping both sts from needle tog.

Pattern Stitch

Wavy Rib

Row 1 (WS): P1, [k3, p1] twice, k1, *p2, k1; rep from * to last 9 sts, p1, [k3, p1] twice.

Row 2 (RS): K1, [p3, k1] twice, p1, *C2F, p1; rep from * to last 9 sts, k1, [p3, k1] twice.

Row 3: P1, [k3, p1] twice, k1, *p2, k1; rep from * to last 9 sts, p1, [k3, p1] twice.

Row 4: K1, [p3, k1] twice, p1, *C2B, p1; rep from * to last 9 sts, k1, [p3, k1] twice.

Rep Rows 1–4 for pat.

Pattern Note

Circular needle is used to accommodate stitches. Do not join; work back and forth in rows.

Dishcloth

Cast on 37 sts.

Border

Row 1 (WS): P1, *k3, p1; rep from * across.

Row 2 (RS): K1, *p3, k1; rep from * across.

Rows 3 and 4: Rep Rows 1 and 2.

Body

Work [Rows 1–4 of Wavy Rib pat] 9 times.

Border

Row 1: P1, *k3, p1; rep from * across.

Row 2: K1, *p3, k1; rep from * across.

Rows 3 and 4: Rep Rows 1 and 2.

Bind off.

Hand Towel
Cast on 73 sts.

Border
Row 1 (WS): P1, *k3, p1; rep from * across.

Row 2 (RS): K1, *p3, k1; rep from * across.

Rows 3–8: Rep [Rows 1 and 2] 3 times.

Body
Work Rows 1–4 of Wavy Rib pat until piece measures about 15 inches, ending with Row 4.

Top
Row 1: P1, [k3, p1] twice, *p2tog; rep from * to last 8 sts, [k3, p1] twice—45 sts.

Row 2: K1, [p3, k1] twice, *k2tog; rep from * to last 8 sts, [p3, k1] twice—31 sts.

Row 3: P1, [k3, p1] twice, knit to last 9 sts, p1, [k3, p1] twice.

Row 4: [K1, p3] twice, knit to last 8 sts, [p3, k1] twice.

continued on page 41

House of White Birches, Berne, Indiana 46711   AnniesAttic.com

Mock-Cable Rib Hand Towel

Design by Sue Childress

Skill Level

◖■■□ INTERMEDIATE

Finished Size
19 x 22 inches

Materials
- Reynolds Saucy (worsted weight; 100% cotton; 185 yds/100g per ball): 2 balls green #555
- Size 9 (5.5mm) 24-inch circular needle
- 1½-inch button

Gauge
16 sts = 4 inches/10cm in St st.
To save time, take time to check gauge.

Special Abbreviation
Cross 2 Back (C2B): Knit into the back of 2nd st on LH needle, then knit into the first st, slipping both sts off needle tog.

4 MEDIUM

Pattern Stitch
Mock-Cable Rib

Row 1 (RS): K4, p2, *k2, p2; rep from * to last 4 sts, k4.

Row 2 and all even-number rows: K6, *p2, k2; rep from * to last 4 sts, k4.

Row 3: K4, p2, *C2B, p2; rep from * to last 4 sts, k4.

Row 5: K4, p2; *k2, p2; rep from * to last 4 sts, k4.

Row 7: K4, p2, *k2tog, but do not slip off needle, knit the first st again, slipping both sts off needle tog, p2; rep from * to last 4 sts, k4.

Row 8: K6, *p2, k2; rep from * to last 4 sts, k4.

Rep Rows 1–8 for pat.

Pattern Note
Circular needle is used to accommodate stitches. Do not join; work back and forth in rows.

Hand Towel
Cast on 82 sts. Knit 8 rows.

Work [Rows 1–8 of Mock-Cable Rib pat] 9 times.

Top
Row 1 (RS): K4, p2tog, *k2, p2tog; rep from * to last 4 sts, k4—63 sts.

Row 2: K5, p2tog, *k1, p2tog; rep from * to last 5 sts, k5—45 sts.

Row 3: K5, *k2tog; rep from * to last 4 sts, k4—27 sts.

Row 4: K4, purl to last 4 sts, k4.

Row 5: Knit.

Rows 6–19: Rep [Rows 4 and 5] 7 times.

Row 20: K1, *k2tog; rep from * across—14 sts.

Rows 21–31: Knit.

Row 32: K5, bind off 4 sts for buttonhole, k5 (includes loop on needle after bind-off).

Row 33: K2tog, k3, cast on 4 sts, k3, k2tog—12 sts.

Row 34: K2tog, k8, k2tog.

Bind off.

Sew button below Row 20. ❖

House of White Birches, Berne, Indiana 46711   AnniesAttic.com

Chevron Rib Place Mat

Design by Sue Childress

Skill Level
◖◼◻◻ EASY

Finished Size
15 x 20 inches

Materials
- Plymouth Fantasy Naturale (worsted weight; 100% cotton; 140 yds/100g per skeins): 3 skeins gray/coral multi #9258
- Size 9 (5.5mm) 24-inch circular needle

Gauge
16 sts and 18 rows = 4 inches/10cm in St st.
To save time, take time to check gauge.

Pattern Stitch
Chevron Rib

Row 1 (WS): K1, p1, k1, p2, *k1, p2, k2, p2, k1, p1; rep from * to last 4 sts, [p1, k1] twice.

Row 2 (RS): [P1, k1] twice, *k3, p2, k2, p2, k1, [p2, k2] twice; rep from * to last 5 sts, k2, p1, k1, p1.

Row 3: [K1, p1] twice, *[p2, k2] twice, p3, k2, p2, k2, p1; rep from * to last 5 sts, p2, k1, p1, k1.

Row 4: [P1, k1] twice, *k1, p2, k2, p2, k5, p2, k2, p2; rep from * to last 5 sts, k2, p1, k1, p1.

Rep Rows 1–4 for pat.

Pattern Notes
Yarn amount is sufficient to make 2 place mats.

Circular needle is used to accommodate stitches. Do not join; work back and forth in rows.

Place Mat
Cast on 81 sts.

Border
Row 1 (WS): K1, *p1, k1; rep from * across.

Row 2 (RS): P1, *k1, p1; rep from * across.

Rep [Rows 1 and 2] twice.

Body
Rep Rows 1–4 of Chevron Rib pat until piece measures about 13 inches, ending with Row 4.

continued on page 41

House of White Birches, Berne, Indiana 46711   AnniesAttic.com

Medallion Rib Place Mats & Napkin Rings

Designs by Frances Hughes

Skill Level
■■■□ INTERMEDIATE

Finished Sizes
Place Mat: 14 x 18 inches
Napkin Ring: 1½ x 6 inches, before seaming

Materials
- Plymouth Fantasy Naturale (worsted weight; 100% cotton; 140 yds/100g per skein): 3 skeins yellow #1242
- Size 9 (5.5mm) 24-inch circular and straight needles or size needed to obtain gauge

Gauge
16 sts = 4 inches/10cm in St st.
To save time, take time to check gauge.

Special Abbreviation
Cross 2 Back (C2B): Knit in back on 2nd st of LH needle, then knit in front of first st, slipping both sts off needle tog.

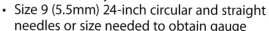

Pattern Stitch
Medallion Rib

Row 1 (RS): [K1, p1] twice, p4, *sl 2p wyib, C2B, p4; rep from * to last 4 sts, [k1, p1] twice.

Row 2: [P1, k1] twice, k4, *sl 2p wyif, purl 2nd st on LH needle, then purl first st, slipping both sts off needle tog, k4; rep from * to last 4 sts, [p1, k1] twice.

Row 3: [K1, p1] twice, knit to last 4 sts, [k1, p1] twice.

Row 4: [P1, k1] twice, purl to last 4 sts, [p1, k1] twice.

Rep Rows 1–4 for pat.

Pattern Notes
Yarn amount is sufficient to make 2 place mats and 2 napkin rings.

Circular needle is used to accommodate stitches. Do not join; work back and forth in rows.

Place Mat
Make 2

Cast on 76 sts.

Border
Row 1: *K1, p1; rep from * across.

Row 2: *P1, k1; rep from * across.

Rows 3 and 4: Rep Rows 1 and 2.

Body
Work Rows 1–4 of Medallion Rib pat until piece measures about 13 inches.

Border
Row 1: *P1, k1; rep from * across.

Row 2: *K1, p1; rep from * across.

Rows 3 and 4: Rep Rows 1 and 2.

Bind off.

Napkin Ring
Make 2

Cast on 8 sts.

Row 1: K1, p1, sl 2p wyib, C2B, k1, p1.

Row 2: P1, k1, sl 2p wyif, purl 2nd st on LH needle, then purl first st, slipping both sts off needle tog, p1, k1.

Row 3: K1, p1, k5, p1.

Row 4: P1, k1, p5, k1.

Rep [Rows 1–4] 6 times.

Bind off.

Sew cast-on and bound-off ends tog. ❖

House of White Birches, Berne, Indiana 46711   AnniesAttic.com

Hourglass Rib Coasters & Glass Jackets

Designs by Sue Childress

Skill Level

■□■□□ EASY

Finished Sizes

Coaster: 5 inches square
Glass Jacket: 3 inches tall x 8½ inches around

Materials

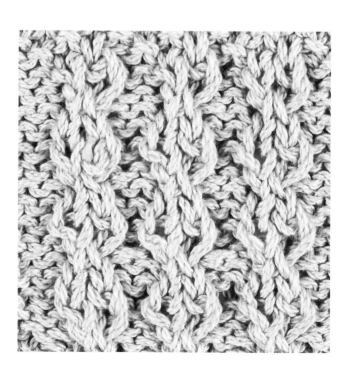

- Reynolds Saucy (worsted weight; 100% cotton; 185 yds/100g per ball): 1 ball pink #396
- Size 9 (5.5mm) needles or size needed to obtain gauge

Gauge

16 sts = 4 inches/10cm in St st.
To save time, take time to check gauge.

Pattern Stitch

Hourglass Rib

Note: St count inc by 1 st per rep on Row 3; original count is restored on Row 4.

Row 1: [K1, p1] twice, k2, *p2, k2; rep from * to last 4 sts, [k1, p1] twice.

Row 2 (RS): [P1, k1] twice, p2, *k2tog-tbl, then knit same 2 sts tog through front loops, p2; rep from * to last 4 sts, [p1, k1] twice.

Row 3: [K1, p1] twice, p2, *p1, yo, p1, k2; rep from * to last 4 sts, [k1, p1] twice.

Row 4: [P1, k1] twice, p2, *ssk, k1, p2; rep from * to last 4 sts, [p1, k1] twice.

Rep Rows 1–4 for pat.

Pattern Note

One ball of yarn will make 4 coasters and 4 glass jackets.

Coaster

Cast on 22 sts.

Border

Row 1: *K1, p1; rep from * across.

Row 2: *P1, k1; rep from * across.

Rows 3 and 4: Rep Rows 1 and 2.

Body

Work [Rows 1–4 of Hourglass Rib pat] 4 times.

Border

Row 1: *K1, p1; rep from * across.

Row 2: *P1, k1; rep from * across.

Rows 3 and 4: Rep Rows 1 and 2.

Bind off.

Wet-block, if desired, shaping to measurements.

To wet-block: Wet item completely with water, roll in a towel to remove excess moisture. Place flat, shaping to measurements. Let dry completely.

Glass Jacket
Cast on 32 sts.

Border
Row 1: *K1, p1; rep from * across.

Row 2: *P1, k1; rep from * across.

Body
Row 1: *P2, k2; rep from * across.

Row 2 (RS): *P2, k2tog-tbl, then knit same 2 sts tog through front loops; rep from * across.

Row 3: *P1, yo, p1, k2; rep from * across—40 sts.

Row 4: *P2, skp, k1; rep from * across.

Rows 5–12: Rep [Rows 1–4] twice.

Row 13: *K1, p1; rep from * across.

Bind off in pat. Finish off leaving an 18-inch end. Sew side edges tog. ❖

Cluster Rib Tablecloth

Design by Sue Childress

Skill Level

 EASY

Finished Size

34 inches square, after wet blocking

Materials

- Universal Yarn Cotton Supreme (worsted weight; 100% cotton; 180 yds/ 100g per skein): 4 skeins beige #504
- Size 10 (6mm) 29-inch circular needle or size needed to obtain gauge
- Stitch markers

4 MEDIUM

Gauge

16 sts and 16 rows = 4 inches/10cm in St st.
To save time, take time to check gauge.

Pattern Stitch

Cluster Rib

Row 1 (RS): K21, p1, *k2, p1; rep from * to last 21 sts, k21.

Row 2: P21, k1, *yo, k2, pass yo over 2 knit sts, k1; rep from * to last 21 sts, p21.

Row 3: K1, [sl 1p wyib, k1] 10 times, p1, *k2, p1; rep from * across to last 21 sts, k1, [sl 1p, k1] 10 times.

Row 4: K1, [sl 1p wyif, k1] 10 times, k1, *yo, k2, pass yo over 2 knit sts, k1; rep from * to last 21 sts, k1, [sl 1p wyif, k1] 10 times.

Row 5: K21, p1, *k2, p1; rep from * to last 21 sts, k21.

Row 6: P21, k1, *yo, k2, pass yo over 2 knit sts, k1; rep from * to last 21 sts, p21.

Row 7: K2, [sl 1p wyib, k1] 9 times, k1, p1, *k2, p1; rep from * to last 21 sts, k2, [sl 1p wyib, k1] 9 times, k1.

Row 8: K2, [sl 1p wyif, k1] 9 times, k2, *yo, k2, pass yo over the 2 knit sts, k1; rep from * to last 21 sts, k2, [sl 1p wyif, k1] 9 times, k1.

Rep Rows 1–8 for pat.

Pattern Note

Circular needle is used to accommodate stitches. Do not join; work back and forth in rows.

Tablecloth

Cast on 133 sts.

Border

Row 1 (RS): Knit across.

Row 2: Purl across.

Row 3: K1, *sl 1p wyib, k1; rep from * across.

Row 4: K1, *sl 1p wyif, k1; rep from * across.

Rows 5 and 6: Rep Rows 1 and 2.

Row 7: K1, *sl 1p wyib, k1; rep from * to last st, k1.

Row 8: K2, *sl 1p wyif, k1; rep from * to last st, k1.

Rep [Rows 1–8] twice.

Body

Work Rows 1 and 8 of Cluster Rib pat until tablecloth measures about 31 inches.

Border
Rep [Rows 1–8 of border] 3 times.

Next row: Knit across.

Next row: Purl across.

Bind off.

Wet-block to measurements.

To wet-block: Wet item completely with water, roll in a towel to remove excess moisture. Place flat, shaping to measurements. Let dry completely. ❖

House of White Birches, Berne, Indiana 46711   AnniesAttic.com

Single-Eyelet Rib Table Runner

Design by Sue Childress

Skill Level

 EASY

Finished Size

15 x 42 inches

Materials

- Katia Cotton Comfort (DK weight; 84% combed cotton/16% nylon; 164 yds/ 50g per ball): 3 balls off-white #3
- Size 7 (4.5mm) needles or size needed to obtain gauge

3 LIGHT

Gauge

22 sts and 28 rows = 4 inches/10cm in pat.
To save time, take time to check gauge.

Pattern Stitch

Single-Eyelet Rib

Row 1 (RS): P1, [k2, p1] twice, p2, *k3, p2; rep from * across to last 7 sts, p1, [k2, p1] twice.

Row 2: K1, [p2, k1] twice, k2, *p3, k2; rep from * to last 7 sts, k1, [p2, k1] twice.

Row 3: P1, [k2, p1] twice, p2, *k2tog, yo, k1, p2; rep from * to last 7 sts, p1, [k2, p1] twice.

Row 4: K9, *p3, k2; rep from * to last 7 sts, k7.

Row 5: P1, [k2, p1] twice, p2, *k3, p2; rep from * to last 7 sts, p1, [k2, p1] twice.

Row 6: K1, [p2, k1] twice, k2, *p3, k2; rep from * to last 7 sts, k1, [p2, k1] twice.

Row 7: P1, [k2, p1] twice, p2, *k1, yo, ssk, p2; rep from * to last 7 sts, p1, [k2, p1] twice.

Row 8: K9, *p3, k2; rep from * to last 7 sts, k7.

Rep Rows 1–8 for pat.

Table Runner

Cast on 91 sts.

Border

Row 1: P1, *k2, p1; rep from * across.

Row 2: K1, *p2, k1; rep from * across.

Row 3: Rep Row 1.

Row 4: Knit.

Rep Rows 1–4.

Body

Work Rows 1–8 of Single-Eyelet Rib pat until piece measures about 41 inches.

Border

Row 1: P1, *k2, p1; rep from * across.

Row 2: K1, *p2, k1; rep from * across.

Row 3: Rep Row 1.

Row 4: Knit.

Rep Rows 1–3. Bind off.

Wet-block.

To wet-block: Wet item completely with water, roll in a towel to remove excess moisture. Place flat, shaping to measurements. Let dry completely. ❖

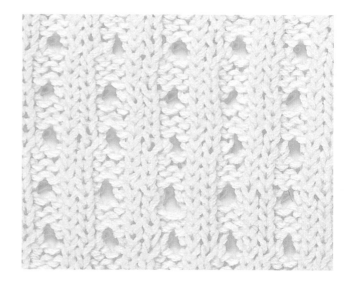

Bobble Rib Runner & Hot Mat

Designs by Frances Hughes

Skill Level

◼◼◻◻ EASY

Finished Sizes

Runner: 20 x 28 inches, after wet-blocking
Hot Mat: 10 inches square

Materials

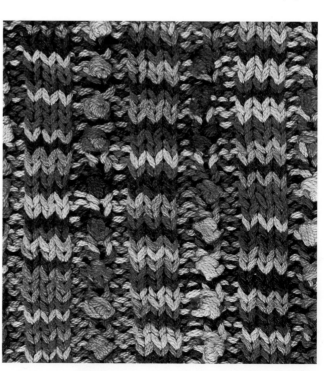

- Plymouth Fantasy Naturale (worsted weight; 100% cotton; 140 yds/100g per skein): 4 skeins shades of blue #9172
- Size 8 (5mm) 24-inch circular needle or size needed to obtain gauge

Gauge

16 sts = 4 inches/10cm in St st.
To save time, take time to check gauge.

Special Abbreviation

Make Bobble (MB): (P1, k1, p1, k1) all in next st, pass first 3 sts 1 at a time over 4th st.

Pattern Stitch

Bobble Rib

Rows 1 (RS) and 2: Knit.

Row 3: K1, *yo, k2tog; rep from * across.

Row 4: Knit.

Row 5: K1, yo, k2tog, *p2, MB, p2, k3; rep from * to last 8 sts, p2, MB, p2, k2tog, yo, k1.

Row 6: K5, *p1, k2, p3, k2; rep from * to last 6 sts, p1, k5.

Row 7: K1, yo, k2tog, *p2, k1, p2, k3; rep from * to last 8 sts, p2, k1, p2, k2tog, yo, k1.

Row 8: K5, *p1, k2, p3, k2; rep from * to last 6 sts, p1, k5.

Rep Rows 1–8 for pat.

Runner

Cast on 75 sts.

Work Rows 1–4 of Bobble Rib pat.

Work Rows 5–8 of Bobble Rib pat until piece measures about 25 inches.

Rep Rows 1–4 of Bobble Rib pat. Bind off.

Wet-block.

To wet-block: Wet item completely with water, roll in a towel to remove excess moisture. Place flat, shaping to measurements. Let dry completely.

Hot Mat

Cast on 35 sts.

Border

Work Rows 1–4 of Bobble Rib pat.

continued on page 41

Pretty Posies Tea Cozy

Design by Frances Hughes

Skill Level

■■■□ INTERMEDIATE

Finished Size

Fits 7-inch high x 9½-inch spout-to-handle teapot

Materials

- Plymouth Fantasy Naturale (worsted weight; 100% cotton; 140 yds/100g per skein): 1 skein pastel multi #9993 (MC) and small amount blue #2576 (A), #3077 pink (B), #1242 yellow (C) and #5425 green (D)
- Size 6 (4mm) double-point needles (for I-cord)
- Size 7 (4.25mm) needles
- Size 8 (5mm) needles or size needed to obtain gauge
- 2 sets of snaps
- Sewing needle and thread

Gauge

16 sts = 4 inches/10cm in St st on size 8 needles.
To save time, take time to check gauge.

Special Abbreviation

Knit in front and back (kfb): Knit in front and back of next st to inc 1 st.

Pattern Note

Before starting cozy, wind a portion of main color (MC) into a 2nd ball of yarn.

Tea Cozy

Lid

Beg at top with MC and size 7 needles, cast on 15 sts.

Rows 1, 3, 5 and 7: Knit.

Row 2: *K1, kfb; rep from * to last st, k1—22 sts.

Row 4: *K1, kfb; rep from * across—33 sts.

Row 6: *K1, kfb; rep from * to last st, k1—49 sts.

Row 8: *K2, kfb; rep from * to last st, kfb—66 sts.

Row 9: Knit.

Change to size 8 needles.

Body

Row 1 (RS): *P1, k1, p1, [yo, p3tog, yo, p1, k1, p1] 5 times; join 2nd ball of yarn and rep from * across rem sts.

Row 2: *K1, p1, k1, [p3, k1, p1, k1] 5 times; rep from * with 2nd ball.

Row 3: *P1, k1, p1, [k3, p1, k1, p1] 5 times; rep from * with 2nd ball.

Row 4: *K1, p1, k1, [p3, k1, p1, k1] 5 times; rep from * with 2nd ball.

Rep [Rows 1–4] 5 times or until piece measures 6 inches from cast-on edge.

Next row: *P1, k1, p1, [yo, p3tog, yo, p1, k1, p1] 5 times; rep from * with 2nd ball.

Change to size 7 needles.

Joining row: Knit across both pieces with same ball of yarn. Cut 2nd ball.

Next row: Knit across.

Next row: *K2, k2tog; rep from * to last 2 sts, k2tog—49 sts.

Next row: Knit across.

Next row: *K1, k2tog; rep from * to last st, k1—33 sts.

Next row: Knit across. Bind off.

Sew joined edge as necessary to fit spout. Sew other seam from cast-on edge through Row 9 of lid. Sew 1 snap on lower garter edge. Sew 2nd snap 2 inches above first.

Leaves

Make 2

With size 7 needles and D, cast on 3 sts.

Row 1: Knit across.

Row 2 and all even-number rows: Purl across.

Row 3: K1, yo, k1, yo, k1—5 sts.

Row 5: K2, yo, k1-tbl, yo, k2—7 sts.

Row 7: K3, yo, k1-tbl, yo, k3—9 sts.

Row 9: Knit.

Row 11: Ssk, knit to last 2 sts, k2tog—7 sts.

Row 13: Ssk, knit to last 2 sts, k2tog—5 sts.

Row 15: Ssk, knit to last 2 sts, k2tog—3 sts.

Row 17: Sk2p.

Large Flower

With size 7 needles and C, cast on 35 sts. Work 8 rows in rev St st. Cut yarn, leaving a 10-inch end. Weave end through sts and draw up tightly. With purl side as RS, twist to form a flower.

Small Flower

Make 1 each pink & blue

With size 7 needles, cast on 25 sts. Work 6 rows in rev St st. Cut yarn, leaving a 10-inch end. Weave end through sts and draw up tightly. With purl side as RS, twist to form a flower.

I-Cord

With 2 double-point needles and D, cast on 4 sts. *K4, slide sts to opposite end of needle, draw yarn across back; rep from * until I-cord measures 14 inches. Bind off. Beg and ending at center of 1 side, sew along Row 9, adjusting length as necessary.

With double-point needles and D, cast on 4 sts. *K4, slide sts to opposite end of needle, draw yarn across back; rep from * until I-cord measures 17 inches. Bind off. Sew a leaf to each end of cord. Form a bow and tack beneath joining of first I-cord.

Referring to photo, place flowers in a bunch on top of bow. ❖

Cable & Eyelet Rib Afghan

Continued from page 4

Afghan
Cast on 124 sts.

Border
Rows 1 and 2: *K2, p2; rep from * across.

Rows 3 and 4: *P2, k2; rep from * across.

Rep [Rows 1–4] 3 times.

Body
Work [Rows 1–8 of Cable & Eyelet Rib pat] 22 times.

Border
Rows 1 and 2: *K2, p2; rep from * across.

Rows 3 and 4: *P2, k2; rep from * across.

Rep [Rows 1–4] 3 times.

Bind off loosely in pat. ❖

Wavy Rib Hand Towel & Dishcloth

Continued from page 23

Rows 5–12: Rep [Rows 3 and 4] 4 times.

Row 13: *P2tog; rep from * to last st, p1—16 sts.

Row 14: K1, *k2tog, k1; rep from * across—11 sts.

Rows 15–31: Knit across.

Row 32: K4, bind off 3 sts for buttonhole, k4 (includes loop from last bind-off).

Row 33: K4, cast on 3 sts, k4.

Row 34: K2tog, k7, k2tog—9 sts.

Row 35: K2tog, k5, k2tog—7 sts.

Row 36: K2tog, k3, k2tog—5 sts.

Bind off.

Sew button on Row 14. ❖

Chevron Rib Place Mat

Continued from page 27

Border
Row 1: K1, *p1, k1; rep from * across.

Row 2: P1, *k1, p1; rep from * across.

Rep [Rows 1 and 2] twice.

Wet-block to measurements.

To wet-block: Wet item completely with water, roll in a towel to remove excess moisture. Place flat, shaping to measurements. Let dry completely. ❖

Bobble Rib Runner & Hot Mat

Continued from page 36

Body
Rep Rows 5–8 of Bobble Rib pat until piece measures about 9 inches.

Border
Row 1: K1, yo, k2tog, *p2, MB, p2, k3; rep from * to last 8 sts, p2, MB, p2, k2tog, yo, k1.

Row 2: Knit.

Row 3: K1, *yo, k2tog; rep from * across.

Rows 4 and 5: Knit.

Bind off. ❖

Knitting Basics

Cast On

Leaving an end about an inch long for each stitch to be cast on, make a slip knot on the right needle.

Place the thumb and index finger of your left hand between the yarn ends with the long yarn end over your thumb, and the strand from the skein over your index finger. Close your other fingers over the strands to hold them against your palm. Spread your thumb and index fingers apart and draw the yarn into a "V."

Place the needle in front of the strand around your thumb and bring it underneath this strand. Carry the needle over and under the strand on your index finger.

Draw through loop on thumb.

Drop the loop from your thumb and draw up the strand to form a stitch on the needle.

Repeat until you have cast on the number of stitches indicated in the pattern. Remember to count the beginning slip knot as a stitch.

Cable Cast-On

This type of cast-on is used when adding stitches in the middle or at the end of a row.

Make a slip knot on the left needle. Knit a stitch in this knot and place it on the left needle. Insert the right needle between the last two stitches on the left needle. Knit a stitch and place it on the left needle. Repeat for each stitch needed.

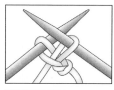

Knit (k)

Insert tip of right needle from front to back in next stitch on left needle.

Bring yarn under and over the tip of the right needle.

Pull yarn loop through the stitch with right needle point.

Slide the stitch off the left needle. The new stitch is on the right needle.

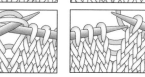

Purl (p)

With yarn in front, insert tip of right needle from back to front through next stitch on the left needle. Bring yarn around the right needle counterclockwise. With right needle, draw yarn back through the stitch.

Slide the stitch off the left needle. The new stitch is on the right needle.

Bind Off

Binding off (knit)

Knit first two stitches on left needle. Insert tip of left needle into first stitch worked on right needle and pull it over the second stitch and completely off the needle.

Knit the next stitch and repeat. When one stitch remains on right needle, cut yarn and draw tail through last stitch to fasten off.

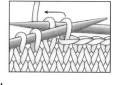

Binding off (purl)

Purl first two stitches on left needle. Insert tip of left needle into first stitch worked on right needle and pull it over the second stitch and completely off the needle.

Purl the next stitch and repeat. When one stitch remains on right needle, cut yarn and draw tail through last stitch to fasten off.

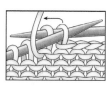

Increase (inc)

Two stitches in one stitch

Increase (knit)

Knit the next stitch in the usual manner, but don't remove the stitch from the left needle. Place right needle behind left needle and knit again into the back of the same stitch. Slip original stitch off left needle.

Increase (purl)

Purl the next stitch in the usual manner, but don't remove the stitch from the left needle. Place right needle behind left needle and purl again into the back of the same stitch. Slip original stitch off left needle.

Invisible Increase (M1)

There are several ways to make or increase one stitch.

Make 1 with Left Twist (M1L)

Insert left needle from front to back under the horizontal loop between the last stitch worked and next stitch on left needle.

With right needle, knit into the back of this loop.

To make this increase on the purl side, insert left needle in same manner and purl into the back of the loop.

Make 1 with Right Twist (M1R)

Insert left needle from back to front under the horizontal loop between the last stitch worked and next stitch on left needle.

With right needle, knit into the front of this loop.

To make this increase on the purl side, insert left needle in same manner and purl into the front of the loop.

Make 1 with Backward Loop over the right needle

With your thumb, make a loop over the right needle.

Slip the loop from your thumb onto the needle and pull to tighten.

Make 1 in top of stitch below

Insert tip of right needle into the stitch on left needle one row below.

Knit this stitch, then knit the stitch on the left needle.

Decrease (dec)

Knit 2 together (k2tog)

Put tip of right needle through next two stitches on left needle as to knit. Knit these two stitches as one.

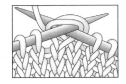

Purl 2 together (p2tog)

Put tip of right needle through next two stitches on left needle as to purl. Purl these two stitches as one.

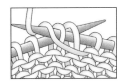

Slip, Slip, Knit (ssk)

Slip next two stitches, one at a time, as to knit from left needle to right needle.

Insert left needle in front of both stitches and work off needle together.

Slip, Slip, Purl (ssp)

Slip next two stitches, one at a time, as to knit from left needle to right needle. Slip these stitches back onto left needle keeping them twisted. Purl these two stitches together through back loops.

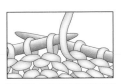

House of White Birches, Berne, Indiana 46711   AnniesAttic.com

Standard Abbreviations

[ ] work instructions within brackets as many times as directed

( ) work instructions within parentheses in the place directed

** repeat instructions following the asterisks as directed

* repeat instructions following the single asterisk as directed

" inch(es)

approx approximately

beg begin/begins/beginning

CC contrasting color

ch chain stitch

cm centimeter(s)

cn cable needle

dec decrease/decreases/decreasing

dpn(s) double-point needle(s)

g gram(s)

inc increase/increases/increasing

k knit

k2tog knit 2 stitches together

kwise knitwise

LH left hand

m meter(s)

M1 make one stitch

MC main color

mm millimeter(s)

oz ounce(s)

p purl

pat(s) pattern(s)

p2tog purl 2 stitches together

psso pass slipped stitch over

p2sso pass 2 slipped stitches over

pwise purlwise

rem remain/remains/remaining

rep repeat(s)

rev St st reverse stockinette stitch

RH right hand

rnd(s) round(s)

RS right side

skp slip, knit, pass slipped stitch over—one stitch decreased

sk2p slip 1, knit 2 together, pass slip stitch over the knit 2 together—2 stitches have been decreased

sl slip

sl 1k slip 1 knitwise

sl 1p slip 1 purlwise

sl st slip stitch(es)

ssk slip, slip, knit these 2 stitches together—a decrease

st(s) stitch(es)

St st stockinette stitch/stocking stitch

tbl through back loop(s)

tog together

WS wrong side

wyib with yarn in back

wyif with yarn in front

yd(s) yard(s)

yfwd yarn forward

yo yarn over

Standard Yarn Weight System

Categories of yarn, gauge ranges, and recommended needle sizes

Yarn Weight Symbol & Category Names	1 SUPER FINE	2 FINE	3 LIGHT	4 MEDIUM	5 BULKY	6 SUPER BULKY
Type of Yarns in Category	Sock, Fingering, Baby	Sport, Baby	DK, Light Worsted	Worsted, Afghan, Aran	Chunky, Craft, Rug	Super Chunky, Roving
Knit Gauge Range* in Stockinette Stitch to 4 inches	27–32 sts	23–26 sts	21–24 sts	16–20 sts	12–15 sts	6–11 sts
Recommended Needle in Metric Size Range	2.25–3.25mm	3.25–3.75mm	3.75–4.5mm	4.5–5.5mm	5.5–8mm	8mm and larger
Recommended Needle U.S. Size Range	1 to 3	3 to 5	5 to 7	7 to 9	9 to 11	11 and larger

* GUIDELINES ONLY: The above reflect the most commonly used gauges and needle sizes for specific yarn categories.

Knitting Needle Conversion Chart

U.S.	1	2	3	4	5	6	7	8	9	10	10½	11	13	15	17	19	35	50
Continental-mm	2.25	2.75	3.25	3.5	3.75	4	4.5	5	5.5	6	6.5	8	9	10	12	15	19	25

Inches into Millimetres & Centimetres

All measurements are rounded off slightly.

inches	mm	cm	inches	cm	inches	cm	inches	cm	inches	cm
⅛	3	0.3	3	7.5	13	33.0	26	66.0	39	99.0
¼	6	0.6	3½	9.0	14	35.5	27	68.5	40	101.5
⅜	10	1.0	4	10.0	15	38.0	28	71.0	41	104.0
½	13	1.3	4½	11.5	16	40.5	29	73.5	42	106.5
⅝	15	1.5	5	12.5	17	43.0	30	76.0	43	109.0
¾	20	2.0	5½	14	18	46.0	31	79.0	44	112.0
⅞	22	2.2	6	15.0	19	48.5	32	81.5	45	114.5
1	25	2.5	7	18.0	20	51.0	33	84.0	46	117.0
1¼	32	3.8	8	20.5	21	53.5	34	86.5	47	119.5
1½	38	3.8	9	23.0	22	56.0	35	89.0	48	122.0
1¾	45	4.5	10	25.5	23	58.5	36	91.5	49	124.5
2	50	5.0	11	28.0	24	61.0	37	94.0	50	127.0
2½	65	6.5	12	30.5	25	63.5	38	96.5		

Skill Levels

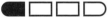

BEGINNER

Beginner projects for first-time knitters using basic stitches. Minimal shaping.

EASY

Easy projects using basic stitches, repetitive stitch patterns, simple color changes, and simple shaping and finishing.

INTERMEDIATE

Intermediate projects with a variety of stitches, mid-level shaping and finishing.

EXPERIENCED

Experienced projects using advanced techniques and stitches, detailed shaping and refined finishing.

House of White Birches, Berne, Indiana 46711   AnniesAttic.com

Photo Index

4

20

7

10

8

12

18

16

14

E-mail: Customer_Service@whitebirches.com

HOUSE of WHITE BIRCHES
PUBLISHERS SINCE 1947

Rib It Up is published by DRG, 306 East Parr Road, Berne, IN 46711, telephone (260) 589-4000. Printed in USA. Copyright © 2010 DRG. All rights reserved. This publication may not be reproduced in part or in whole without written permission from the publisher.

RETAIL STORES: If you would like to carry this pattern book or any other DRG publications, call the Wholesale Department at Annie's Attic to set up a direct account: (903) 636-4303. Also, request a complete listing of publications available from DRG.

Every effort has been made to ensure that the instructions in this pattern book are complete and accurate. We cannot, however, take responsibility for human error, typographical mistakes or variations in individual work.

STAFF

Editor: Jeanne Stauffer
Assistant Editors: Kortney Barile, Stephanie Timm
Technical Editor: Kathy Wesley
Technical Artist: Nicole Gage
Copy Supervisor: Michelle Beck
Copy Editor: Amanda Scheerer
Graphic Arts Supervisor: Erin Augsburger

Graphic Artists: Debby Keel, Amanda Treharn
Art Director: Brad Snow
Assistant Art Director: Nick Pierce
Photography Supervisor: Tammy Christian
Photography: Matthew Owen
Photo Stylist: Tammy Steiner

ISBN: 978-1-59217-276-4
1 2 3 4 5 6 7 8 9